P9-DBP-382

Blairsville Junior High School
Blairsville, Pennsylvania

THE FREEDOM OF THE PRESS IN AMERICA

The IN AMERICA *Series*

THE FREEDOM OF THE PRESS
IN AMERICA

DAVID J. GOLDMAN

Published by
Lerner Publications Company
Minneapolis, Minnesota

32.3.44
Hol

To Adam

Copyright © 1967 by Lerner Publications Company

All rights reserved — no part of this book may be reproduced in
any form without permission in writing from the publisher,
except for the inclusion of brief quotations in a review.

International Copyright Secured. Printed in U.S.A.

Library of Congress Catalog Card Number: 67-15682

...CONTENTS...

A newspaper dies, "in hopes of a resurrection to life again." The English Parliament's Stamp Act of 1765 imposed a tax upon all stamped paper, including that used for newspapers. Lacking funds to pay the tax, many colonial newspapers had to suspend publication. Editor William Bradford included an essay on liberty in this edition of *The Pennsylvania Journal,* October 31, 1765.

PART I

The Importance of Freedom of the Press

1. *The Bill of Rights*

The citizens of the United States are among the freest in the world. This liberty, which most of us take for granted, did not happen by accident. It was carefully planned by the founders of our nation. If it is not understood and guarded by all generations, it could be lost. Even though the guarantees in the Constitution and its amendments, the Bill of Rights, sound absolute, they only say that we have certain freedoms. The framers of these two documents could not anticipate, and thus provide for the handling of, every situation that would arise in the future. The Constitution and the Bill of Rights insure that our country is as free as the people want it to be.

When the 13 original states met to ratify the Constitution, 12 of them wanted it to list specifically certain rights which Congress could not take away from the people. They agreed to ratify on the condition that the first Congress would immediately amend the Constitution to include these rights. James Madison drew up 12 amendments, 10 of which were approved by Congress and ratified by the states. In 1791 the 10 amendments, known as the Bill of Rights, became part of the law of the land.

2. *The First Amendment*

The First Amendment states that:

> Congress shall make no law respecting an establishment of religion, or prohibiting the free exercise thereof; or abridging the freedom of speech, or of the press; or the right of the people peaceably to assemble, and to petition the Government for a redress of grievances.

This book is about one of the most important of our freedoms: freedom of the press. Freedom of the press does not mean only freedom to write and print — it includes other methods of spreading ideas and news, such as radio broadcasts, television programs, and motion pictures.

Freedom of the press is closely related to the other basic freedoms that were included with it in the First Amendment. On First Amendment liberties rest the right to worship according to our beliefs, to act and think freely about political matters, and to gain knowledge and communicate with people.

Freedom of the press is necessary so that people can find out about the many different ideas, events, and opinions of others. With this opportunity they can decide for themselves what is true and valuable.

Freedom of the press is also necessary so that the people can know what their leaders are doing.

Finally, it is a guarantee that every person may publicly criticize or praise the government, churches, schools, and other institutions. Without freedom of the press we could not sustain a democratic way of life.

PART II

World History

1. *Freedom in Ancient Civilizations*

The idea that man should be able to express himself freely was recorded as early as the fifth century B.C. in the works of Greek and Roman orators and writers. The playwright, Euripides, wrote: "This is true liberty when free-born men, having to advise the public, may speak free."

From Socrates, the great philosopher of ancient Greece, came what is probably the first recorded argument that the value of free discussion is not only for the speaker, but also for the whole community. Socrates wanted to help the citizens of Athens think for themselves instead of accepting ideas simply because everyone else accepted them. Each morning at sunrise, Socrates would roam the streets of the city, stopping people to ask them to discuss their opinions. As Socrates asked individuals to explain the ideas they accepted as truth, he made them realize that they did not really know if their opinions were correct.

Euripides (480-406 B. C.), Greek playwright whose tragedies included political and social criticism. Euripides was a close friend of Socrates.

9

Some influential citizens of Athens thought that Socrates' questions ridiculed them. They joined with his political enemies to invent charges that would silence him.

Socrates argued in his own defense to a jury of 501 citizens of Athens. His defense gave many reasons for the importance of freedom of expression. He warned the jury that, if he were sentenced to death, the people of Athens would not easily find another person to make them think. "If you put me to death," Socrates said, "you will not injure me more than your own selves. I am far from defending myself for my own sake; but for your sake I do it…"

Despite his plea, the jury sentenced Socrates to death, but his arguments for freedom of expression, recorded by his pupil Plato, are still used today.

Though there were a few men in ancient Greece and Rome who argued for freedom of expression, their number was very small and their ideas of the meaning of freedom of expression were very different from current American ideas. The liberty to say what one thought was granted only to those few people who were considered citizens. Even among citizens the authors of two kinds of writing were punished—those who wrote evil accounts of the living or dead, and those who wrote critical or mocking words about the gods.

Socrates receives the cup of poisonous hemlock. Athens, 399 B. C. (Painting by Jacques-Louis David, 1787. Metropolitan Museum of Art)

Sir Thomas More (1478-1535), author, scholar, and Lord Chancellor of England under King Henry VIII. More was beheaded when he refused to acknowledge Henry's control of the English church. Protestants and Catholics alike were victims of the Reformation, in an age when toleration of many beliefs was rarely considered possible.

2. *The Struggle for Religious Freedom*

After the fall of the Roman Empire, in the fifth century A.D., there is no record of men having argued for freedom of expression on anything but religious matters for more than 1,000 years.

In the fourth century A.D. the people began a practice which was to last into the seventeenth century — the hunting out and persecution of heretics. Heretics are church members who hold beliefs opposed to official church doctrine. In the ninth century church officials joined the practice by writing the punishment of heretics into church law. There could be no question of freedom of discussion while men were afraid to express their religious beliefs even in front of their neighbors.

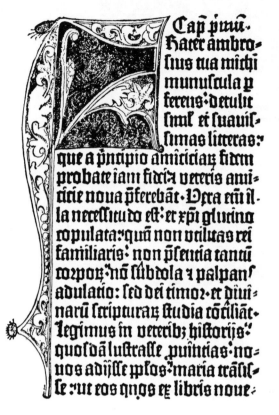

A facsimile of the first page of Gutenberg's bible (left) and (above) the printer's device of William Caxton.

In the early sixteenth century there was a religious revolution called the Reformation which divided western Christianity into Protestant and Catholic churches. In each country, the church with the help of the government told everyone exactly what to believe and how they must worship. This was especially difficult for the people of England, where the official religion changed with each king or queen. The Reformation made freedom of religion an issue for everyone. Many men and women who had not previously given much thought to freedom of discussion now realized its importance. Most of them, however, wanted free discussion only for those who believed as they did.

3. *The Press...Its Beginning*

About 1459 Johann Gutenberg of Germany developed printing from movable type. The invention made it possible for new ideas to spread more quickly than ever before. The introduction of new ideas was looked upon as a threat by those in power. Before long the Catholic Church in Rome ruled that all printers had to be licensed.

4. *The Press in England*

The first printing press in England was set up by William Caxton in 1477. Caxton translated foreign books, printing them in English. He also printed old English literature which he first translated into the language as it was spoken in his time. His work was supported by the King, and noblemen helped finance the printing.

William Caxton, the first English printer, shows printed proofs to King Edward IV. Modern publishers have printed facsimiles of some of Caxton's beautiful editions of the classics.

5. *Press Censorship in England*

With the Reformation, printers became feared and distrusted, and the support of the nobility ceased. Although the English church was independent of Rome, all printed material was strictly controlled. Only a small number of printers were granted the license which gave them permission to print. Even licensed printers were required to have any material they wanted to publish approved by an official censor.

In early seventeenth century England anyone caught printing without approval was arrested and brought before the Star Chamber. The Star Chamber, a small group of the King's friends and advisors, acted as a court with no jury. Its penalties were

Charles I of England (1600-1649), from a painting by Anthony Van Dyke. The forces of Parliament defeated Charles's armies in the civil wars of 1642-1645, and Charles was beheaded in 1649.

severe. Chamber members were particularly hard on anyone who offended the King. For example, in 1632, a lawyer named William Prynne published a book criticizing the theater. Since King Charles I and his Queen enjoyed the theater, this book was considered an attack on them. The Star Chamber sentenced the author to life imprisonment, fined him a large sum, cut off his ears, and burned all of the copies of his book they could find. The Star Chamber was abolished by Parliament in 1641 but censorship remained.

Despite arrests, cruel punishments, and the destruction of presses, secret presses kept appearing. Seventeenth century England was flooded with unsigned pamphlets. While these pamphlets expressed their authors' ideas on many lively topics, few of them appealed for freedom of expression. One which did, however, was given little notice in its author's lifetime, but is often quoted today. The author was the poet John Milton, and the pamphlet was published without a license in 1644. Titled *Areopagitica*, it was a plea to Parliament to abolish the licensing of printing. Milton argued that the strength of truth should be relied upon. He said, "Let her [Truth] and Falsehood grapple; who ever knew Truth put to worse in a free and open encounter."

Milton also said that there are very few books which are completely bad. When a censor bans a book which contains what he considers to be a few bad parts, all of the good parts and all new ideas are lost.

Censorship by licensing ended in 1694, half a century after Milton's plea. This meant that the work of writers and printers no longer needed to be approved before publication. But soon after licensing ended the government controlled printing by the law of seditious libel. This law made it a crime for authors and printers to publish anything that might bring hatred or contempt against the king or the government. It was also a crime to write or print anything that would cause subjects to try in an illegal way to change any rule of church or state, or to stir up discontent among the king's subjects. The law was written in language which was so unclear that any criticism of the government or its policies could be considered a violation. From the eighteenth century point of view, the greater the truth, the greater the libel. This meant that publishing a story about a dishonest official was more seditious if the official actually was dishonest.

The right to report was almost as hard to win as the right to criticize. Reporting an official's actions, or even a debate in Parliament, could be decreed seditious libel. Reporting of parliamentary proceedings was banned until 1771.

6. *The Demand for News Grows*

By the early part of the seventeenth century the people of England had become more interested in what was happening in their own country and throughout Europe. England had become a leading sea power, social conditions within the country were growing better, and the Thirty Years' War was being fought on the Continent between Protestants and Catholics.

In 1621 the demand for news encouraged three men to produce a newsbook on a weekly basis. Called a *coranto,* this publication was the first of its kind. It contained translated items from the news-sheets of Europe. All corantos were suppressed in 1632 because some of them contained news which offended the Spanish Ambassador. After the Star Chamber was abolished, weekly publications containing news of English matters appeared, and in 1702 the first daily paper was published. Popular "essay" papers were also started. Many people learned to read and helped spread the news to those who could not.

The eighteenth century press was controlled by the law of seditious libel, but the very existence of the press promoted freedom. For just as freedom of religion is necessary before man can be truly free, so is freedom from ignorance. A people with no knowledge of the world or its affairs must depend on men of authority to tell them what to do and what is right or true. As man's knowledge grew so did his desire for freedom.

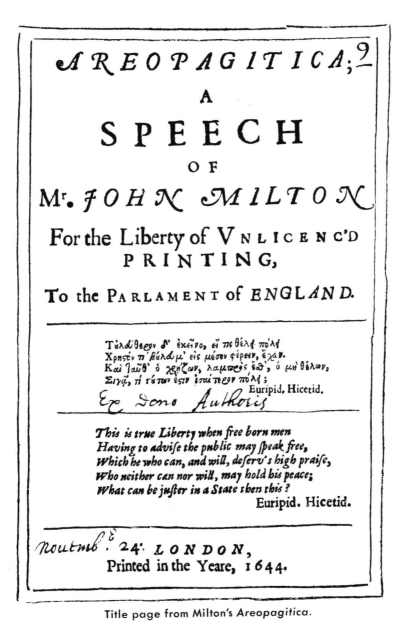

AREOPAGITICA; 9

A

SPEECH

OF

Mr. *JOHN MILTON*

For the Liberty of Vnlicenc'd
PRINTING,

To the Parlament of ENGLAND.

Τἀλεύθερον δ᾽ ἐκεῖνο, εἴ τις θέλει πόλει
Χρηστόν τι βούλευμ᾽ εἰς μέσον φέρειν, ἔχων.
Καὶ ταῦθ᾽ ὁ χρῄζων, λαμπρός ἐσθ᾽, ὁ μὴ θέλων,
Σιγᾷ. Τί τούτων ἔστ᾽ ἰσαίτερον πόλει;
Euripid, Hicetid.

Ex Dono Authoris

This is true Liberty when free born men
Having to advise the public may speak free,
Which he who can, and will, deserv's high praise,
Who neither can nor will, may hold his peace;
What can be juster in a State then this?
Euripid. Hicetid.

Noemb. 24. *LONDON,*
Printed in the Yeare, 1644.

Title page from Milton's Areopagitica.

PART III

Colonial America

1. *Censorship*

Printing in colonial America was even more strictly regulated than in England. Although prior censorship (censorship before publication) ended in England in 1694, it continued to be enforced in the Colonies for another 25 years.

Besides licensing laws and libel prosecutions, the English government had another way of controlling the colonial press: a rule that printing presses and type could not be manufactured in the Colonies. The secret presses of seventeenth century England could not exist in America during that century.

2. *Colonial Printing Presses*

The first press was brought to New England by Harvard College and the Puritans in 1638. Between that time and the Revolution each of the 13 colonial governments furnished money for presses. These presses were used to publish almanacs, textbooks, legal forms, and government laws. The "Publick Printer" was an aid to the colonial government. He did not criticize the government or even print anything controversial.

3. *The First Newspapers*

Fifty years after the first press was brought to New England an attempt was made to establish the first American newspaper.

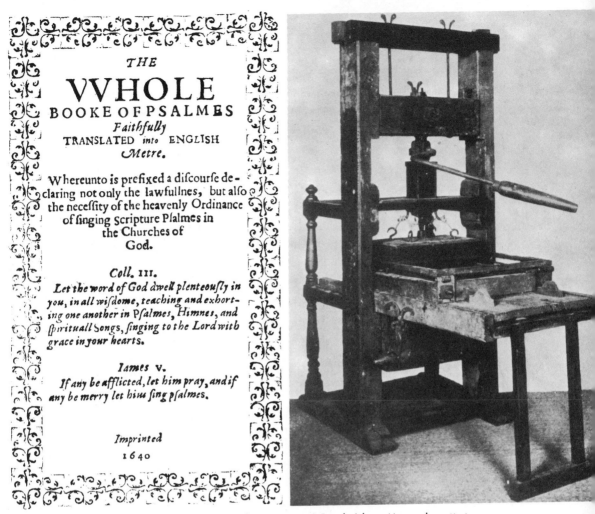

THE

VVHOLE
BOOKE OF PSALMES
Faithfully
TRANSLATED *into* ENGLISH
Metre.

Whereunto is prefixed a difcourfe de-
claring not only the lawfullnes, but alfo
the neceffity of the heavenly Ordinance
of finging Scripture Pfalmes in
the Churches of
God.

Coll. III.

*Let the word of God dwell plenteoufly in
you, in all wifdome, teaching and exhort-
ing one another in Pfalmes, Himnes, and
fpirituall Songs, finging to the Lord with
grace in your hearts.*

Iames v.

*If any be afflicted, let him pray, and if
any be merry let him fing pfalmes.*

Imprinted
1 6 4 0

In 1638 Stephen Daye and his son Matthew came to Cambridge, Massachusetts to set up the first printing press in British North America (right). The earliest surviving book from the press was *The Whole Book of Psalmes*, usually known as *The Bay Psalm Book*, of 1640.

Published in Boston by a former London bookseller and publisher, Benjamin Harris, the paper was titled *Publick Occurrences Both Forreign and Domestick*. The paper was to be published once a month ("or if any Glut of Occurrences happen, oftener"). Four days after its publication the Massachussets governor and council ordered that, since Harris had no license, he could not continue to publish his newspaper. Massachussetts authorities were not so much angered by the fact that *Publick Occurrences* had no license as by the fact that it contained some gossip about the King of France. They were also offended by an account of events in the French and Indian War which told of the torture of French captives by some Indian allies of the English.

Fourteen years later the first continuously published American paper, the *Boston News-Letter,* appeared. The publisher, Boston postmaster John Campbell, didn't take the chance that Harris had taken. He went to the authorities for advance censorship before he published anything. The *News-Letter* continued to be published by various men for 72 years. It was one of the three longest-lived eighteenth century colonial papers.

Probably the first colonial newspaper to defy civil and re- ligious authorities was the *New-England Courant,* which first appeared on August 7, 1721. Its printer was James Franklin, older brother of Benjamin. Although it lasted less than six years, it introduced readers to a new kind of journalism. The paper was bold and witty. Its criticism of those in authority, especially Puritan religious leaders Increase Mather and his son, Cotton, delighted most readers. But when the *Courant* treated the government's defense against pirates humorously, the Royal Council had James Franklin put in prison. While James was in prison his brother Benjamin published the paper in much the same manner as before. Once out of jail James Franklin again displeased the colonial government and was forbidden to publish any pamphlet or news- paper. He defied that order by naming Benjamin as publisher. The paper remained entertaining but not nearly as daring as it had been.

Gradually, through the years, newspapers were developed in other colonies. Until the time of the Revolution, however, only a few of these papers were free to print anything critical about

New-England.   Numb. 776

The Boston News-Letter.

Published by Authority.

From **Monday** February 23. to **Monday** March 2. 1719.

Paris, December 8. 1717.

THE Printed Appeal of the Cardinal de Noailles is privately handed about, and makes a great Noise. It bears Date the 3d of April last, and 'tis mentioned therein, that 11 Bishops have adher'd thereto, viz. the Bishop of Chalons Sur Marne, Leon, Auxerre, Macon, Condom, Agen, Bayonne, Dax, St. Malo, Metz, and the late Bishop of Leitoure, amongst whose Papers, 'tis said, a Copy of this Appeal was found. The same has been sent to Rome, and 'tis believed it will exasperate that Court, but it will be very difficult to perswade that the Cardinal and the other Appealing Bishops did not secretly connive at the publishing of this Appeal. The Parliament has thought fit to issue out an Arrest forbidding the selling of the said Appeal, and ordered the same to be suppress'd. On Saturday Night, or rather Sunday Morning, there was a great Tumult before the Hotel of Soissons, where the Ambassador of Sicily gave a great Ball, and 4 Persons were killed on the spot. The same Day there was another Tumult in the House of the Ambassador of Spain, who holds Assemblies, where People game very high, and at the same thing has happened at the Imperial Ambassador's, and that frequent Murders are committed in the Publick Gaming Houses, we hear an Arrest is to come out to forbid these Practices.

B.2il, Decemb. 8. The Abbot of St. Gall departed this Life on the 28th past, near Lindaw on the Lake of Constance, in the 78th Year of his Age.

Paris, Decemb. 10. The Earl of Peterborough having been dismissed by the Cardinal Legate of Bologna, arrived here on the 10th Instant. Letters from Naples advise, that Count Dann had ordered the Pope's Nuncio to depart that City in 24 Hours, and the Kingdom in 48, which Order had been punctually observed. This Week the Duke of Queensberry arrived here. Letters from the Captain General Pisani, give an Account of his being arrived at Corfu with the Fleet, having left Prevesa and Venice well provided with all Necessaries, and that General Schulenbourgh has extended the Contributions beyond Arta.

Paris, Decemb. 11. The Arrest of our Parliament for suppressing the Appeal of the Cardinal Noailles is made publick, and bears date the 1st of this Month. The Motives of that Suppression are contained in the Speech made by the King's Advocate General, in the Name of the King's Council, importing, That they saw with Grief, that in Contempt of the Declaration of the 7th of October last, which suspends all the Disputed and Contests form'd in the Kingdom, on Occasion of the late Constitution of our most Holy Father the Pope, there are lately spread in this City, many Copies of a Writing, entituled, The Act of Appeal of his Eminence Monseigneur the Cardinal de Noailles, Archbishop of Paris, &c. Printed without the Allowance or Participation of that Prelate. That an Impression made in such Circumstances, could not be other than the Work of seditious People, who employ themselves only in sowing Trouble and Division in the Church, whilst a Prince, more to be respected for his Virtues, and for his Zeal for the Interest of Religion, than for his high Station and high Birth, employs incessantly all his Cares for establishing a Calm. They cannot therefore forbear claiming the Authority of the Court, against a Publication so contrary to the late Declaration of the King; and that in order, to maintain so wise a Law, they believ'd themselves oblig'd to draw up the Conclusions in Writing, which they delivered accordingly, with the Printed Copy of the Appeal. The King's Council being retired, the Court examin'd the said Writing, entituled, An Act of Appeal, of his Eminence Monseigneur the Cardinal de Noailles, Archbishop of Paris, of the 3d of April 1717. to the Pope, better advised, and to a future General Council, from the Constitution of our Holy Father the Pope Clement XI. of the 8th of September 1713. and the King's

Declaration of the 7th of October, Register'd in Parliament. And the Matter being put into Deliberation, the Court ordered, that the Copies of the said Print shall be suppress'd, &c. All Persons are forbid selling, publishing or distributing the same, upon the Penalties express'd in the said Declaration of October 7th. And it is ordered that the said Declaration shall be observed and executed in it's full Form and Tenor, &c.

The Partisans of the Bull are not very well pleased with this Arrest, because it confirms People that it is the Genuine Appeal of the Cardinal de Noailles, which some People doubted of before, seeing the Publication of it without the Licence of the Cardinal, and the Contempt of the Edict, forbidding to write or publish in Publick any thing about the Constitution, are the only Motives of this Arrest of the Parliament. That Act of Appeal is very long, and the Cardinal sets forth therein, the pernicious Consequences that all sorts of People draw from the said Constitution, to weaken the most essential Truths of the Christian Faith, and undermine the Foundations of Morality, and declares that he has in vain endeavoured for 3 Years together to obtain from the Pope such Explanations as might prevent these Consequences; concluding, that he finds himself under an unavoidable Necessity to appeal to the Pope, better advised, and the future General Council freely assembled in a safe Place where he or his Deputies may safely appear, from the Constitution Unigenitus, and all other Proceedings made in Consequence thereof.

Rome, Decemb. 11. The Expulsion of our Nuncio from Naples, and the Demands made since by the Imperial Court, embarrass very much the Pontiff, which appears sufficiently by the first great Congregations that have been lately held; but we do not hear that they are come to any other Resolution, but only to endeavour to pacify the Emperor, who has been perswaded that this Court has not sincerely dealt with him, and has under-hand favoured the designs of King Philip. They complain that the promise made by the Pope upon the Invasion of Sardinia, to recal his Nuncio from Madrid, for having not given him Notice of the Projects of that Court, of which there is a strong Suspicion, if not a clear Evidence, that he was informed: was a great Imposition upon the Imperial Court, and a new insufferable Provocation, since that Minister continued there, and has not put a stop as it was promised, to the raising of the Tenth Penny Tax on all the Ecclesiastical Revenues; but rather conceived at the Continuation thereof, tho' they cannot be ignorant that that Money, which was employed to disturb the Peace of Europe, and assist the Turks against the Christians, by giving a Diversion to the Imperial Forces. They complain on the other hand of the Partiality of the Pope, who readily granted that Tax to the Court of Madrid, whereas he started a World of Difficulties, when the Emperor demanded the like Contribution from the Clergy of Naples and Milan, tho' it was evident, that Supply could not be employed to any other use but against the Turks, with whom his Imperial Majesty was actually engag'd in War. They seem perswaded, that the Report we had some time ago of a League between Spain and some Italian Princes, to drive the Imperialists out of Italy, were not groundless, and that the unexpected Defence of the Marquish de Rabi in Sardinia, having taken up the Spaniards till the fair Season was almost over, the Powers concerned in that League did not break off, but only defer'd to a more favourable Opportunity, in which they are confirmed by the great Preparations of the Court of Madrid, and their Manifestoes; in which they alledge some Grievances of the Italian Princes, as one of their Reasons for invading the Imperial Territories.

Hamburgh, Decemb. 14. The King of Poland set out the 1st Instant from Dresden to return into his Kingdom, and has left the Administration of his Electorate to Count Fleming as Stadtholder thereof, which is very acceptable to the Saxons, that Minister having on all Occasions, given Proofs of his Zeal for the Protestant Religion. Letters from Petersburgh say, that the Czar

---

The Boston News-Letter, February 23, 1719 — a detailed, gossipy account of world news, from Paris, Venice, Rome, and Hamburg, all of it datelined December. Founded in 1704, the *News-Letter* was the first American paper to survive its initial printing.

the government. Even during the time of the Revolution newspapers were only free if they agreed with public opinion. Thus, the *Boston News-Letter* went out of business in the early days of the Revolution because its publishers remained loyal to the British.

A continental bill from the press of James Franklin, 1776.

4. *The Trial of John Peter Zenger*

The trial of John Peter Zenger was one of the most important events in the early history of the struggle for a free press in this country.

Zenger was the printer of the *New York Weekly Journal,* a paper whose writers and financial supporters were opposed to the administration of British Governor William Cosby. Many of the colony's leading citizens agreed with the articles that Zenger printed against Cosby and his council. They disliked the governor's arbitrary and dictatorial actions. The *Journal* began publication in 1733. A year later the governor and his council had four issues publicly burned. When this didn't stop the attacks, Zenger was imprisoned. Although he was kept in prison for nearly 10 months, only one issue of the paper was missed. Zenger's wife, Anna Catherine, got instructions about running the print shop through a hole in the prison door, and the paper came out each Monday.

Zenger was charged with attempting to bring Governor Cosby and other officials into suspicion and the ill opinion of the people — seditious libel.

Governor Cosby thought he was certain to get a verdict against Zenger. He had personally picked his court officials — Chief Justice James Delancy and Associate Justice Frederick Philipse. Attorney General Franklin Bradley explained the old law of seditious libel to the jury. He told them that their only duty was to declare by whom the *Journal* had been printed and who had been libeled. The jury had nothing to do with the verdict, he said — the Court would decide that.

The trial of **John Peter Zenger,** New York City, 1735. Lawyer **Andrew Hamilton** speaks to the jurors: "It is not the bare printing and publishing of a paper that will make it a libel: the words themselves must be libelous, that is, false, scandalous, and seditious, else my client is not guilty."

Zenger was defended by Andrew Hamilton of Philadelphia, one of the colonies' most outstanding lawyers. Hamilton outraged the Chief Justice by speaking to the jury instead of to the judges. He told them that there was no reason for them to be there if they did not give the verdict. He urged them to find Zenger guilty only if the stories in his paper were not true.

Hamilton spoke eloquently to the jury. He said, "The question before the court…is not just the cause of the poor printer…No! It is the best cause, it is the cause of liberty…the liberty both of exposing and opposing arbitrary power…by speaking and writing truth."

The jury ignored Attorney General Bradley's instructions that the verdict was not their affair. They found John Peter Zenger not guilty, on the grounds that the articles he had printed were true.

The Zenger trial was a step toward freedom for colonial Americans in three ways. It proved that the people could successfully protest against government officials. It gave meaning to the jury as a group of ordinary citizens who could decide a verdict. It established that printed criticism of the government or its officials was not a crime if the criticism was true.

PART IV

The Press and the Revolution

The flames of the American Revolution were fed by a group of able writers who used the pen and the press to arouse people to action.

1. *The Stamp Act*

The Stamp Act of 1765 required that all books, newspapers, official papers, and legal documents be written on officially stamped paper for which a special tax had to be paid. The tax was especially hard on colonial newspaper publishers as it took a large share of their profits. Some had to temporarily suspend publication. Others got around the law by printing their newspapers as handbills. There were some papers, however, that printed bitter criticism of the Act. Two of the most outspoken were the *Boston Gazette* and the *Massachusetts Spy*. Samuel Adams, writing for the *Gazette*, went much further than simply protesting the Stamp Act. He used the Act to talk about political freedom, insisting that every man is born free. His articles for the *Gazette* inspired many Americans.

The Stamp Act was repealed within a year of its passage. It had been defeated by the open revolt of the colonial press.

2. *The Penman of the Revolution*

Another journalist who aided the revolutionary cause was John Dickinson, the "Penman of the Revolution." Dickinson's series of articles, published in the *Pennsylvania Chronicle* in 1767 and 1768, were entitled "Letters from a Farmer in Pennsylvania to the Inhabitants of the British Colonies." He was protesting the Townshend Acts, which were the attempt of the British Government to levy taxes upon colonial Americans when the Stamp Act

25

Blairsville Junior High School
Blairsville, Pennsylvania

The Stamp Act of 1765 was, indirectly, a means of limiting freedom of the press. Here, angry colonists burn the stamped paper.

failed. Dickinson argued that government should be controlled by constitutional law. His words "Let these truths be indelibly impressed on our minds: that we cannot be happy without being free..." were reprinted in most of the colonial newspapers. Dickinson was not arguing for independence from England—he was arguing for freedom from taxation by Parliament.

John Dickinson (1732-1808) wrote a series of articles protesting the Townshend Acts of 1767, which levied a tax upon certain imports. Colonists considered the tariff as objectionable as the Stamp Act. Parliament repealed the Acts in 1770, retaining only the tax on tea.

3. *Thomas Paine*

During the years just before the Revolution, many colonists were speaking out for political freedom but few called for an actual separation from England. Opinions were very confused when Thomas Paine arrived in Philadelphia from England in 1774. The injustices he had seen in England and the struggle there for freedom were fresh in his mind. He had read much about man's natural rights and he believed that Americans could only have those rights by separating from England. On January 10, 1776, his pamphlet *Common Sense* appeared. It was a clear call to the American colonists to fight for separation. Paine spoke of the natural rights of men and of the duty of all governments to protect men of all religious beliefs. He said "...until an independence is declared, the continent will feel itself like a man who continues putting off some unpleasant business from day to day, yet knows it must be done..."

Thomas Paine (1737-1809) wrote *Common Sense* in 1776 and, during the war, a series of pamphlets called *The Crisis*. Paine was a political and religious dissenter. His pamphlets were a source of encouragement to the leaders of the American Revolution, but he died in poverty and social neglect.

27

Within three months after it was published, 120,000 copies of *Common Sense* had been sold. It had an immediate effect, causing thousands of people to favor independence.

When separation from England became the desire of the majority, rather than of a few extremists, the colonies declared their independence, in July 1776.

The long and often discouraging war against the British was won in 1783. The power of a free press in molding the opinions of men and freeing them from tyrants was now clear. When the founders of the new American nation were meeting to write its constitution, there were no debates about freedom of the press — it was something everyone wanted.

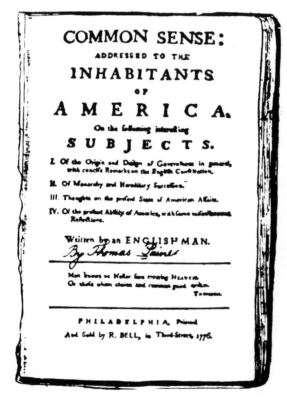

Title page of *Common Sense*. Thomas Paine's pamphlet demanded independence from England and the formation of a new federal government. The pamphlet was printed without the author's name.

PART V

Freedom of the Press in the United States: the First Problems

1. *The Right to Report*

The House of Representatives was open to reporters in 1789, just two days after it had organized itself. The Senate, however, admitted only reporters from local papers until 1846. It was soon obvious that, while the First Amendment guaranteed freedom of the press, no one knew exactly what the guarantee meant. They did know that prior censorship, or censorship before printing, was a thing of the past except in cases of protecting the country during wartime. Aside from that, the words of the First Amendment, "Congress shall make no law…abridging the freedom of speech, or of the press…" meant different things to different people.

2. *The Alien and Sedition Acts of 1798*

The great statesmen who led the new government during its first decade were sharply divided on how it should be governed. The Federalists, led by Alexander Hamilton, thought the country would benefit most under the leadership of men of education, wealth, and high social position. The Republicans (today's Democratic party) were led by Thomas Jefferson, and believed in government by all of the people.

The newspapers of the day were also sharply divided. Each individual newspaper became the spokesman for one party or the other. The criticism exchanged between the Federalists and the Republicans through newspaper articles was bitter, heated, and often ugly.

In 1798 the Federalists were in power. There was an election coming up in two years and the Federalists thought that their candidate, President John Adams, would suffer because of the criticism he was receiving in the Republican press. They were afraid that Vice-President Thomas Jefferson, with his appeal to the common people, would be elected President.

The country, at that time, was fighting an undeclared war with France, and the Federalists believed that all Republicans were French sympathizers.

Thomas Jefferson (1743-1826). A political struggle between Jefferson's party and the Federalists led to passage of the Alien and Sedition Acts in 1798.

John Adams (1735-1826). His government passed the Alien and Sedition Acts in order to silence Republican criticism. By avoiding war with France, Adams also conflicted with pro-war members of his own party.

The Federalists decided that the Republicans must be silenced. To do this they passed the Alien and Sedition Acts. The Alien Act gave the President the authority to order any alien to leave the country if his words or actions were dangerous to the peace and safety of the United States. The Act provided for no trial or hearing.

The Sedition Act made it a crime to "write, utter, or publish false, scandalous, and malicious criticism against the Federal government, its officials and legislators, or its laws."

In theory only false criticism was to be punished. However, in practice Federalist judges and politicians used the law to harass and punish anti-Federalist editors.

One editor was jailed for printing a letter to the editor which accused President Adams of "ridiculous pomp, foolish adulation, and selfish avarice."

Vice-President Jefferson and James Madison prepared, for their respective states of Kentucky and Virginia, resolutions claiming that the states had the right to nullify an unconstitutional act of Congress, which they believed the Sedition Act to be.

Jefferson had always been a supporter of freedom of the press. In 1787 he had written to a friend:

> I am persuaded that the good sense of the people will always be found to be the best army...The people are the only censors of their governors...The basis of our government being the opinion of the people, the very first object should be to keep that right (full information of government affairs) and were it left to me to decide whether we should have a government without newspapers or newspapers without a government, I should not hesitate a moment to prefer the latter!

Jefferson qualified his statement by adding: "But I mean that every man should receive those papers and be capable of reading them."

The Federalists' plan to quiet their opposition and win the elections had the opposite effect. Public opinion was turned against them and Thomas Jefferson was elected President.

The Alien Act expired in 1800 and the Sedition Act in 1801. There had been no convictions under the Alien Act, but a number of aliens, some of them newspaper editors, left the country in fear when it was passed. President Jefferson pardoned all who had been convicted under the Sedition Act.

As a result of the controversy over the passage of the Alien and Sedition Acts, the American people added to their understanding of the meaning of free speech. The freedom of the press to criticize the government and its officials, without having to prove the criticism is true, has been a part of American tradition ever since.

John C. Calhoun (1782-1850).

PART VI

The Nineteenth Century

1. *Changes in Freedom of the Press*

Freedom of the press did not undergo as great changes in the nineteenth century as it did during the colonial and revolutionary periods.

Congress in 1831 limited the power of federal courts to cite for contempt. It restricted punishable activities to disturbances in court that might threaten to obstruct justice.

In 1836 a vigorous debate over press rights developed in Congress. It came out of the proposal by John Calhoun and other slave-state senators to enact legislation that would empower the Post Office Department to refuse to circulate newspapers or other literature that advocated the abolition of slavery in any state where this circulation was forbidden by law.

Senator Daniel Webster opposed the bill, saying it violated the First Amendment, and Calhoun's bill was defeated.

Although Congress, in defeating John Calhoun's bill, had voted for freedom of the press, the actions of many people showed that they believed the press was free to argue only if it was arguing for a popular cause. On several occasions mobs wrecked and destroyed the presses which printed anti-slavery papers. The worst incident occurred in 1837 when Reverend Elijah P. Lovejoy, the publisher of an abolitionist paper, was murdered by a mob in Alton, Illinois.

Elijah P. Lovejoy (1802-1837), clergyman and editor of the *Alton Observer*, an anti-slavery paper. Lovejoy moved to Illinois after several difficult years in St. Louis, Missouri, where his views were not popular. In Alton, he was killed when he tried to prevent a mob from destroying his new press. Two presses had already been destroyed. *(Portrait courtesy of the Chicago Historical Society)*

Most nineteenth century newspaper editors, however, were free to print what they chose except during wartime.

After the Civil War started in 1861, the Post Office on its own authority refused to deliver certain newspapers that it judged disloyal to the Union. Censorship was also used for news from the battle fronts. It was alternately administered by the departments of State, Treasury, and War.

Relations between Army authorities and newspaper correspondents at the front were not good. The government had obtained the right, under the Articles of War, to prosecute persons spreading information of value to the enemy. Some congressmen charged that the censorship of war news was more concerned with quieting legitimate criticism than with guarding military secrets. Since little was done to threaten the liberties of most northern newspapers this charge would seem to be true.

Again during the Spanish-American War in 1898, there was some censorship governing outgoing telegraph and cable correspondence.

2. *Newspaper Contents Change*

When editors felt free to print whatever they pleased, great changes took place in the style and content of newspapers. After the first quarter of the nineteenth century many people learned to read. As newspaper circulation rose, advertising revenues increased. The newspaper, which had once been produced as the printer's sideline, was becoming a business in itself. A new kind of journalism was attempted, with editors searching for ways to attract more readers.

In 1833 a young New York printer named Benjamin H. Day published America's first successful penny paper. Day's paper began a completely new trend in American journalistic style since it published stories about everyday happenings in the city instead of publishing only political news. The *Sun* was the first American newspaper to regularly cover police court news. American readers were delighted with the *Sun* and the appearance of fresh ideas of what made news.

James Gordon Bennett went further in developing the idea of what was newsworthy. He started the *New York Herald* in 1835. He outdid the *Sun* with even more colorful, lively, inventive stories. Bennett's Wall Street and society stories were the fore-runners of our modern financial and society pages.

In the middle of the nineteenth century two newspapers appeared which set new standards of quality for American journalism. They were the *New York Tribune* and the *New York Times*. These papers attempted to report the news decently and fairly.

James Gordon Bennett, Jr. (1841-1918), son of the founder of the *New York Herald*. His father originated the methods of modern journalism and was the first editor to send reporters out for the news. The younger Bennett, who shared his enthusiasm, became owner of the *Herald* at his father's retirement in 1867. In 1924 the *Herald* merged with the *New York Tribune* (founded by Horace Greeley in 1841) to form the *Herald Tribune*, which died in August 1966.

Joseph Pulitzer (1847-1911) and **William Randolph Hearst** (1863-1951). Pulitzer, an immigrant from Hungary, founded the *St. Louis Post-Dispatch* in 1878. In 1883 he bought the *New York World* and made it a crusading newspaper, which competed for circulation with Hearst's *New York Journal*. Hearst, a wealthy Californian, received the *San Francisco Examiner* as a gift from his father in 1885. His publication empire included 25 large daily newspapers by 1937.

3. *Yellow Journalism*

Near the end of the nineteenth century many American newspapers became filled with abuses and excesses. The type of journalism that became fashionable was called "yellow journalism." It was stimulated in the 1890's by a circulation war between William Randolph Hearst's *New York Journal* and Joseph Pulitzer's *New York World.* In their fight for leadership the *Journal* and the *World* reached great circulation figures by resorting to techniques of sensationalism. The largest and most prominently featured stories were those concerned with crime, divorces, scandal, and gossip. Large headlines were used as well as "faked" pictures and false interviews.

The Fight at Guantanamo, June 14, 1898. During the Spanish-American War, newspapers made extensive use of drawings, whose imaginative qualities could make war appear more exciting and interesting than photographs could.

Both the *Journal* and the *World* found it very profitable to print stories of atrocities committed by Spanish forces in Cuba. They played a large role in bringing America into a war with Spain by insisting that America must fight.

One famous incident is a good illustration of Hearst's behavior. In 1897 fiction writer Richard Harding Davis and artist Frederic Remington were sent by Hearst to Cuba to send back atrocity stories. According to an account by another *Journal* war reporter, James Creelman, Remington found his assigment disagreeable. Supposedly he cabled Hearst that there was no trouble in Cuba, there would be no war, and he desired to return home. Hearst cabled back:

REMINGTON, HAVANA:

PLEASE REMAIN. YOU FURNISH THE PICTURES

AND I'LL FURNISH THE WAR.   HEARST

There is no evidence that Hearst sent this cable, but it shows the limits to which Hearst would go to sell newspapers.

Some newspapers used only a few elements of yellow journalism—for example, the huge headlines. Others moved in new directions. In 1896 Adolph Ochs took over the *New York Times,* determined to put out a well-balanced paper which paid little attention to sensation. In 1898 he lowered the price of the *Times* from three cents to a penny, putting it in competition with the penny yellow journals. With the lowered price and continued excellence, the *Times'* circulation and advertising grew. Ochs proved that a newspaper could avoid sensationalism and still make a huge profit. His success influenced other editors to use his methods instead of Hearst's. Responsibility or irresponsibility in the newspaper business did not depend on the law—people got the kind of journalism they were willing to pay for.

Adolph S. Ochs (1858-1935), manager and later publisher of the *New York Times.* Ochs separated the functions of editorial comment and objective reporting.

Mastheads from major newspapers, **1937.** Mergers and closings have reduced the number of papers in twentieth century **America.** At the turn of the century New York City had 15 dailies, and by the late 1960's, only three.

PART VII

The Twentieth Century

Early in the twentieth century many newspaper editors realized that, because the power of the printed word is so great, it should be used with responsibility. Groups of editors formed associations in which codes of ethics were developed. These editors saw an obligation to give readers honest reporting by resisting outside pressures and avoiding malicious comment.

The techniques of yellow journalism gradually disappeared except for the tabloid newspapers, which first appeared in 1919. A tabloid is a newspaper with a small page size and much space used for pictures. While the early tabloids were "scandal sheets," many of them eventually improved their methods of reporting.

The twentieth century has been a time of mergers of newspapers. Papers have been combined, or have been purchased by larger, more successful ones. As a result there are fewer newspapers and the public has fewer differing opinions from which to choose.

In the twentieth century other forms of communication have developed. Radio, television, and motion pictures are often included in the broad definition of the word *press*.

Above all, in the twentieth century a number of events have caused us to define more clearly what we mean by freedom of the press.

Lincoln Steffens (1866-1936), journalist and reformer. In 1902 Steffens wrote for *McClure's Magazine* the first of a series of articles revealing corruption in city governments. Searching, intensive reports by individual newsmen have been an important function of twentieth century journalism.

1. *Free Speech During World War I*

It was not until 1917, when the United States entered World War I, that the American people realized how little agreement there was about the meaning of freedom of speech and press.

The Espionage Act of 1917 barred from the mails any publication which wilfully attempted to cause disloyalty or to obstruct recruiting.

The Trading-with-the-Enemy Act, also passed by Congress in 1917, required any newspaper or magazine containing articles written in a foreign language to file sworn translations with the local postmaster. America was at war with Germany and this act most affected German-language newspapers, many of which were loyal to Germany. On the other hand a number of English-language newspapers were allowed much freedom in their criticism of the war.

The United States entered World War I on April 6, 1917, and on May 18 Congress passed the Selective Service Act. In many cities, draftees marched in huge parades before leaving for their training camps. The Schenck case arose from an attempt to urge opposition to the draft laws.

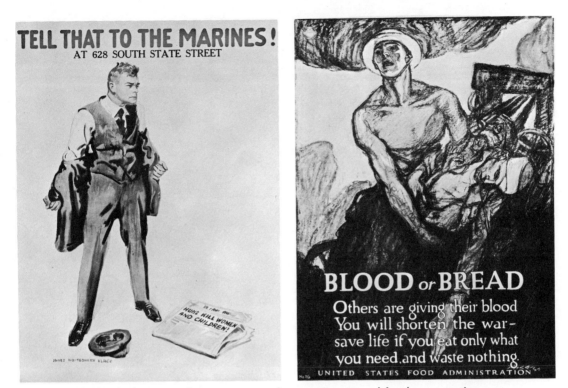

With the declaration of war, programs for recruitment and food conservation were briskly undertaken. Posters appealed for help from the soldier and the housewife; people who questioned the war effort were considered unpatriotic. Responding to this atmosphere, Congress passed the Sedition Act of 1918. (Posters courtesy of the Chicago Historical Society)

Many people feared that speaking or writing against America's war effort could cause us to lose the war. They wrote letters to their congressmen asking for stronger laws. As a result Congress passed the 1918 Sedition Act. This act made it a crime to write or publish any disloyal, profane, or abusive language about the form of government of the United States, the Constitution, the flag, or the military or naval forces. It was also a crime to use any words favoring the cause of any country at war with the United States.

The Masses, founded in 1911, numbered among its contributors John Reed, Sherwood Anderson, and Carl Sandburg, as well as artists John Sloan, Art Young, George Bellows, and Stuart Davis. A magazine of political and social criticism, *The Masses* opposed the war and American participation in it. Acting under the Espionage Act, the Post Office refused to permit the issue of August 1917 to go through the mails, and then suspended the magazine's mailing privileges because it had not maintained continuous publication. *(Magazine covers reproduced by permission of Quadrangle Books from* Echoes of Revolt: The Masses, 1911-1917, *edited by William L. O'Neill, copyright © 1966 by Quadrangle Books, Inc.)*

The Post Office Department used the broad language of the three acts to exercise vast powers. A large number of papers were affected. Some of them could use the mails only by agreeing to print nothing about the war. Others, such as the socialist papers, *New York Call* and *Milwaukee Leader,* and the socialist magazine *The Masses,* were refused mailing privileges. About half of the German-language papers stopped publishing. Three editors of a German-language paper were sent to prision for publishing disloyal articles.

When Congress passed the Sedition Act, some of the state legislatures passed espionage and sedition acts of their own. Anyone expressing an opinion that might be considered disloyal — whether in a newspaper or magazine, in a handbill or pamphlet, or even in a conversation — might be arrested. The hard-won liberty to criticize was lost during this period.

Public protests from distinguished leaders — and the close of the war in November 1918 — caused the use of the Acts to lapse. The Sedition Act of 1918 was repealed in 1921. The Espionage Act remains on the books.

2. *The Supreme Court Interprets Freedom of the Press*

In the period just before World War I most Americans thought that their rights of freedom of speech and the press were firmly established. The arrests made under state and federal espionage and sedition acts caused many to wonder how much freedom they actually had. Before the war it was rare for the Supreme Court to hear a case involving freedom of the press. Starting in 1919, the Court began to hear appeals from some of the people who had been arrested under the wartime laws. Ever since then the Court has struggled with the question of how much freedom of the press is guaranteed by the First Amendment.

In 1925 the Court declared that the Fourteenth Amendment to the Constitution protected freedom of speech and press against violation by state laws. The Fourteenth Amendment, passed after the Civil War, guaranteed that no state could "deprive any person of life, liberty, or property, without due process of law..." The 1925 declaration by the Court meant that liberty of the press and of speech were no longer protected against action by Congress only.

3. *Clear and Present Danger*

The first decision of the Supreme Court in a case arising from a conviction under the 1917 Espionage Act was the case of *Schenck* versus the *United States.* Justice Oliver Wendell Holmes, Jr., speaking for all of the members of the Court, upheld the conviction of individuals who, in a time of national emergency (World War I), had published pamphlets that urged draftees to oppose the nation's draft laws. Justice Holmes said, "The question in every case is whether the words are used in such circumstances and are of such a nature as to create a clear and present danger that they will bring about the substantive evils that Congress has a right to prevent. It is a question of proximity and degree."

What was a "clear and present danger"? This question was to be answered by considering the circumstances of each case. Holmes elaborated the clear and present danger doctrine in another case decided in the fall of 1919.

The case of *Abrams* versus the *United States* originated in the printing and circulating of two leaflets during World War I. They were written by a group of young Russian immigrants who protested the sending of American troops to Russia (in 1918) where a revolution was taking place. They urged a strike of munitions workers, saying that the munitions would be used not only to murder Germans but also Russians.

Since the United States was at war with Germany, a strike of munitions workers would have been very harmful to our war effort. A majority of the justices upheld the conviction of the defendants. Justice Holmes and Justice Louis D. Brandeis did not agree with the other members of the Court. Holmes, in his dissenting opinion, said that it is only the present danger of *immediate evil* or intent to bring it about that warrants Congress in setting a limit to the expression of opinion where private rights are not concerned. "... Congress certainly cannot forbid all effort to change the mind of the country..."

Two decades passed before the majority of Supreme Court Justices came to accept the philosophy that Holmes expressed in the Abrams case. By the 1940's the Court was using the clear and present danger test to help decide cases of freedom of press, speech, and religion. With this philosophy there was much more freedom of the press during World War II than there had been in World War I.

4. *Fear Brings New Suppression*

By mid-century many Americans were alarmed by the growing influence of Communist ideology. Congress passed an Alien Registration Act — the Smith Act of 1940 — the first peacetime sedition act since 1798. This act made it illegal to advocate or teach the doctrine of violent overthrow of any government in the United States. It also made it illegal to print, publish, or distribute any written material advocating the violent overthrow of any government in the United States. In 1951, in the case of *Dennis* versus the *United States,* the Supreme Court handed down its opinion of the constitutionality of the Smith Act. In upholding the Act as applied to 11 leaders of the American Communist Party, Chief Justice Vinson's opinion was: "Overthrow of the government by force and violence is certainly a substantial enough interest for the Government to limit speech." Justice Vinson used a standard suggested by Judge Learned Hand in his Second Circuit Court of Appeals opinion previously handed down on this case: "In each case (courts) must ask whether the gravity of the 'evil,' discounted by its improbability, justified such invasion of free speech as is necessary to avoid the danger." The Court decision was split into a number of opinions, but the majority were in favor of upholding the conviction. To Justice Vinson the clear and present danger test was not appropriate for testing words associated with large-scale plots to overthrow the government.

Six years later, in its opinion on another case, the Court said that it is not illegal to speak or write in favor of the idea of violent

The United States Supreme Court, 1967. Back row: (left to right) Associate Justices Byron R. White, William J. Brennan, Jr., Potter Stewart, and Abe Fortas. Front row: Tom C. Clark, Hugo L. Black, Chief Justice Earl Warren, William O. Douglas, and John M. Harlan. In 1967 Thurgood Marshall was appointed to replace retiring Justice Tom C. Clark.

overthrow of the government. It is illegal, however, to use words to teach action for the overthrow of the government and to prepare people for such action.

The changing opinions of the Supreme Court throughout the years show that freedom of the press depends on the state of world affairs and the state of public opinion in the United States at any particular time.

5. *Censorship by the Post Office*

According to federal law the Post Office Department has the responsibility to keep obscenity out of the mails. It must also bar from the mails material used to conduct a lottery, and fraudulent advertising. The Post Office has given publishers censorship problems. In 1946 the Post Office tried to withdraw the second-class mailing privilege from *Esquire* magazine on the theory that the lower cost of second-class mail was provided for those who make a "special contribution to the public welfare."

Esquire, faced with an additional half-million dollar postal bill, appealed to the Supreme Court. The Court ruled in its favor, saying that "To withdraw the second-class rate from this publication today because its contents seemed to one official not good for the public would sanction withdrawals of the second-class rate tomorrow from another periodical whose social or economic views seemed harmful to another official." The decision reduced the Post Office's role in censorship. The Post Office can refuse to deliver a particular issue of a publication, but it cannot rule on issues that have not yet been printed.

6. *Motion Pictures, Radio, and Television*

The motion picture industry has set up its own code of regulation as a kind of self-censorship, through the Motion Picture Association of America. State and city censorship boards have tried to exercise pre-censorship over movies. Since 1952 these actions have been frequently challenged by the courts as unconstitutional. Other pressures come from religious and civic organizations within the community.

Radio and television, like the press, are not subject to pre-censorship. They, too, have attempted to provide some form of self-censorship. The radio and television industries have had some problems because violations of what is termed "good taste" could result in difficulties with the Federal Communications Commission, which licenses all broadcasting stations.

An early experimental broadcasting station. The first commercial broadcasts in the United States went on the air in 1920, from stations KDKA in Pittsburgh and WWJ in Detroit. Radio stations are licensed by the Federal Communications Commission, which has no powers of censorship.

Radio and television stations are licensed because Americans have decided that the broadcast channels belong to everyone and are thus subject to public control. In 1912 Congress passed its first legislation on broadcasting: the Department of Commerce was to issue licenses to private broadcasters and assign them wave lengths in order to avoid interference with government wave lengths.

During World War I all wireless operations were temporarily brought under the control of the government but were later returned to private hands. As the number of stations increased and confusion over airwaves developed, the radio industry asked the government for help.

In response to this request, Congress passed the Radio Act of 1927. The Act established a five-man commission to regulate radio communications. The government retained control of all channels and granted three-year licenses to broadcasters who would operate "in the public interest, convenience or necessity" and would provide "fair, efficient and equitable service" across the country.

In 1934 federal authority was broadened when a seven-man Federal Communications Commission (FCC) was established with control over all radio and television broadcasting. The license-holder was charged with a responsibility to operate within the "public interest." The Commission was given the power to refuse renewal of a license when it detected an obvious disregard of broadcasting responsibility. However, the FCC rarely uses this power. The law forbids any censorship by the Commission, and no station can be ordered to put particular programs on or off the air.

Radio and television stations are as free as newspapers and magazines to provide the public with whatever news they deem fit to use. While individual commentators are common on radio and television, most station owners have been reluctant to broadcast their own opinions.

In 1941 the FCC issued a ruling that the broadcaster could not support or recommend a particular idea or course of action. Eight years later it decided that stations could "editorialize with fairness." Recent decisions by Congress and the FCC have declared that in political campaigns all candidates must be provided with equal time to present their views. This causes much confusion when it involves minor candidates.

7. *The Right to Criticize*

The right to criticize still needs protection in twentieth century America. In the 1930's Louisiana political boss (and governor) Huey Long tried to punish his newspaper opponents by taxation. Long and his associates put a special tax on the advertising income of larger Louisiana dailies—the papers that opposed Long's administration. The Supreme Court held this tax unconstitutional in the case of *Grosjean* versus the *American Press Company*. The Court said that Long's methods fell within the category of a tax on knowledge, which had been ruled out since the time of the American Revolution.

Huey P. Long (1893-1935) on the campaign trail. Long, who was governor and senator as well as political boss of Louisiana, attempted to tax the state's newspapers in order to punish those which opposed him.

Senator Joseph McCarthy (second from right) conducts an investigation of the U.S. Army Signal Corps at Fort Monmouth, New Jersey, October 1953. The televised Army-McCarthy hearings of May-June 1954 halted the Fort Monmouth investigation and exposed Senator McCarthy's behavior and methods to a viewing public of 20 million people. As a result of the hearings, the Senate voted to censure McCarthy, and his direct influence upon the American government and people was effectively checked.

From 1950 to 1954 all areas of political life in the United States were influenced by Senator Joseph R. McCarthy of Wisconsin. McCarthy's claim that there were more than 200 card-carrying Communists in the State Department resulted in a period of national fear that was greater than any this country had ever experienced. Week after week Senator McCarthy made fresh claims that the Communists were taking over the country. For many Americans no group was free of suspicion — the army, school teachers, labor union members, even church officials. People were afraid to speak out for fear that they would be accused of being pro-Communist. The newspapers and magazines that dared to criticize Senator McCarthy were subject to cancelled subscriptions, harassment, and denunciation. But McCarthy and his many followers were not able to bring about legislation to restrict the long-standing right of the press to criticize public officials.

Contempt of court is the punishable act of showing disrespect for the authority or dignity of a court. In the 1940's a series of Supreme Court decisions broadened the freedom of the newspaper to write about and comment on court cases and the actions of judges. The theory of clear and present danger was applied in the case of *Bridges* versus *California* in 1941. The Court decided that, unless a definite danger to the administration of justice was created by the publication of comment on court proceedings, the newspaper could not be held in contempt.

A photographer is attacked by a bystander (right) at a demonstration. Is there a point at which press coverage becomes an invasion of privacy?

8. *The Press's Access to News*

In this century there is little possibility that newspaper reporters will be denied access to Congressional galleries. However, reporters are admitted to Congressional committee meetings only upon the consent of the chairman and members. State legislatures have similar rules. Radio and television reporters have had a hard time winning access to legislative sessions. They have done so after great persistence, but the freedom to use all of their equipment is frequently restricted.

In a 1966 article, "Television Covers the War," **Morley Safer** (below), CBS News correspondent, revealed the extent of the government's conflict with the press on coverage of the war in Viet Nam. Meeting with Safer and other members of the press in Saigon, in July 1965, Arthur Sylvester, then Assistant Secretary of Defense for Public Affairs, rebuked the newsmen for failing to present the war in an entirely favorable light. But Safer pointed out that press reports have been highly accurate. He said newsmen do not rely upon releases from the government, nor can television hide the painful reality of war.

Reporters are admitted to court sessions only by consent of the judge. Juvenile courts are the most restrictive. Since most trials are public the reporter has as much chance to attend as the average citizen.

Photographers and radio-television men have great difficulty in covering trials. The use of cameras and microphones in the courtroom is banned by the code of ethics of the American Bar Association. These devices are viewed as a hindrance to the proper administration of justice.

An important doctrine concerning the reporting of legislative and judicial affairs is called "qualified privilege." This means that a newspaper is free to report the actions of a legislative body or of a court provided its report is fair and accurate. The doctrine rests on the idea that the press has an obligation to report legislative and judicial sessions to the public. Damaging statements made in legislative sessions and courts can be reported without fear of law suits.

News sources, especially on the local level, are often denied to reporters. Boards of education and city councils often have closed meetings. In the 1950's some states passed "open meeting" laws to enable the press to report important events.

The most publicized denial of access to news has been in the executive departments of the Federal Government. The reason given for the denial is the need for national security. Newsmen and their organizations have fought this trend with only a small degree of success. Some progress was made in 1965 when a House subcommittee, headed by Representative John Moss of California, studied the information policies of government agencies. It forced some reforms by publicizing refusals of the executive department to make available information on public matters.

Recently we have seen good and bad aspects of complete press coverage of public events. When President John F. Kennedy was assassinated in 1963 the general coverage by television, radio,

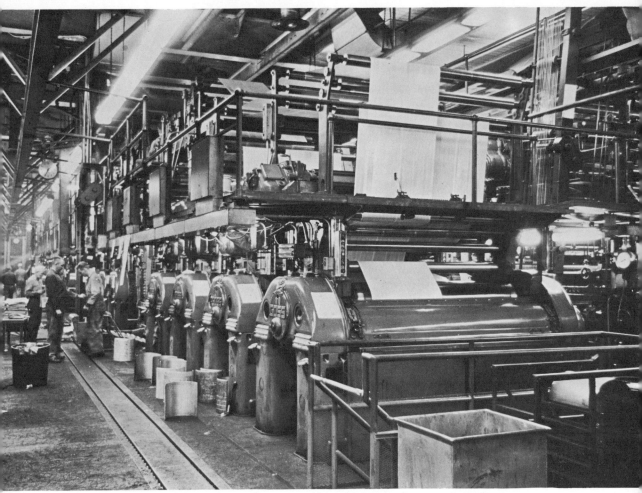

The printing plant of a modern newspaper: high-speed presses in action.

and newspapers was excellent and complete. But the confusion caused by the many newspapermen present two days later, when accused assassin Lee Harvey Oswald was being transferred from one jail to another, was partially responsible for Oswald's being shot by a member of the surrounding crowd. In addition, the press coverage about Oswald's actions, and the many background stories about him, have raised the question of whether he could have received a fair trial, had he lived.

The New York Times, November 25, 1965. Despite excellent press coverage of events related to President Kennedy's death, the publicity might have denied Lee Oswald or Jack Ruby a fair trial, had either of them lived.

Since Oswald's murder, "trial by newspaper and television" has been an important consideration for many lawyers, judges, and others interested in civil liberties. In 1966 the Supreme Court ordered a new trial for Dr. Samuel Sheppard, who had been convicted in 1954 of murdering his wife. The Court said that Dr. Sheppard's trial had been unfair because of the carnival atmosphere caused by unruly press coverage. Americans saw that in this case, as in others, the press is needed to inform us of what is happening in the courtroom—but in order to insure justice for the accused this freedom of the press must be used with responsibility.

Another case heard by the Supreme Court in the 1960's concerned Billie Sol Estes, a financier who had been convicted of swindling and other related offences. In the case of *Estes* versus *Texas* the Supreme Court stated that the televising and broadcasting of a two-day pre-trial hearing and of the actual trial deprived Estes of his right of due process of law under the Fourteenth Amendment. In delivering the majority opinion of the Court, Justice Tom Clark said of pre-trial publicity: "...it may be more harmful than publicity during the trial for it may well set the community opinion as to guilt or innocence..." Justice Clark also said: "The trial witnesses present at the hearing, as well as the original jury panel, were undoubtedly made aware of the peculiar public importance of the case by the press and television coverage being provided, and by the fact that they themselves were televised live and their pictures rebroadcast on the evening show..." The Court ordered that Estes be granted a new trial.

The years of this century have been eventful ones in the story of freedom of the press. Court decisions, social and political changes, and new forms of communication have raised important questions. Freedom of the press has needed to be defined and redefined.

ESTES—PORTRAIT OF A WHEELER-DEALER

Money Lenders Aided His Rise But His Disregard For Them Led Finally to His Downfall

By TOM WICKER

Special to The New York Times

AUSTIN, May 13—Billie Sol Estes is a product of the families and plains of West Texas and he limitless spirit of the American frontier...

"Howdy, pardners . . ."

"Picking up the scent should be easy."

THE BILLIE SOL ESTES CASE

"All the king's men."

"Why-not see what's inside?"

More Than Vision

But there was more to Billie Sol than vision and, imagination...

Heart Counts

What counted was the heart...

ESTES—STORY OF HIS FINANCES

It was the need for hard, cold cash that finally ruined Billie Sol Estes...

Big Pops

Billie Sol had autographed pictures of politicians...

The Big Takeover

Armed with the loan, Billie Sol went for the West Texas liquid fertilizer market...

"Texas stinkweed."

"When buzzards hover."

Big Mistake

That was where Billie Sol made his mistake...

— T. W.

LOOK TO MASSACHUSETTS...

ALL THE INGREDIENTS NEEDED FOR A SUCCESSFUL PLANT "MIX" ARE HERE.

"This $1 million package of facts provides all the answers for executive decision makers."

As Governor of the Commonwealth of Massachusetts, I invite you to explore the unique advantages our state offers many companies. (1147 have come here since 1951.) If our unusual blend of money, brains, skills, and markets might be useful to your business, we would like to send you all the facts.

We have prepared a million dollar package of materials designed to give you an accurate and unvarnished profile of our state.

This package contains a current listing of every manufacturing space for sale or lease in Massachusetts; a comprehensive study of zoning and regional planning in each of our 351 cities and towns; a detailed monograph on any city or town you're interested in; a report of the Massachusetts Business Development Corporation; a location map of the 306 new industries which have grown up just along Route 128 since 1951; a copy of our plain-spoken Commerce Digest; and ample background on our state as a place to live.

If this material could help you now — or if you'd simply like it for future reference — it's yours for the asking. There is no obligation.

For your copy of Massachusetts' Fact Package, simply write, wire or phone LA 3-6640 collect to John T. Burke, Commissioner of Commerce, 150 Causeway Street, Boston, Massachusetts.

JOHN A. VOLPE, Governor

A checklist of assets Massachusetts offers: HOW MANY COULD HELP TO BUILD YOUR BUSINESS?

There are 5M's in Massachusetts:

MONEY · MANPOWER · MARKETS   "New Frontier of the Space Age"
MANAGEMENT · MATERIALS   Dynamic Center of Research and Development

THE NATIONAL OBSERVER SEES MUSIC BOOM

Last year more Americans attended symphony concerts than professional baseball games, and some 32 million people now play musical instruments, said The National Observer recently in its story about the U.S. "cultural explosion."

If you and your family are interested in music and the arts, then say The National Observer, the culturally rich new weekly newspaper from Dow Jones & Co. Covers national and world affairs, science, social trends, theater, music, TV and radio, books, business, cooking, sports. Enjoy this wonderful new weekly now.

The National Observer costs $10 a year, but you can't get a Trial Subscription for 16 weeks for $3.60. Just send this ad with check for $3.60 Or tell us to bill you. Address: The National Observer, 1013 14th St., N.W., Washington 3, D.C.

Procurement problems?

Here is a way of life that's packed full of enjoyment every day for every member of the family. "Our ability to attract top people is certainly based in good part on the ideal living conditions found in the Valley of the Sun." — J. J. O'Brien, vice president and general manager, Allen-Bradley Co. of Arizona. (AiResearch has increased its Phoenix staff from 170 to 2800 since 1951.)

All this, plus: No bonded state debt, award-winning city government, no manufacturers' inventory tax, rapid equipment depreciation for tax assessment purposes, free port law, ample supply of skilled and semi-skilled labor, low dispersion and longrange, productive man-hours.

OPPORTUNITY IS THE MOST POPULAR COMMODITY IN SOUTH JERSEY

Overwhelmed by the projected price of expansion? Hesitating to make the necessary move because of distribution problems plus the reluctance of key personnel to transfer far afield?

Why not relocate in Southern New Jersey. Enjoy overnight shipping to 3/4 of the U.S. population. Find diversified labor, favorable zoning, ...healthy business climate plus low-cost natural gas keep overhead low. Picturesque suburban, rural communities offer gracious living with nearby recreation. Write for full details, Site Map.

SOUTH JERSEY GAS CO.
Atlantic City, New Jersey
Member of the Southern New Jersey Development Council

Phoenix ARIZONA

The New York Times, May 13, 1962: background articles about Billie Sol Estes, with a sample of political cartoons from other newspapers. The Estes case became a test in the conflict between freedom of the press and the right to a fair trial.

PART VIII

Protection Against Libel

1. *The Average Citizen*

The press in our country does not have the right to print reckless, false, or malicious information which might damage the reputation of an average citizen. Each of the 50 states and the District of Columbia has libel laws to protect its citizens from irresponsible journalism.

Since the libel laws differ in each state, libel can be written about only in general terms. It is safe to say that it is against the law to write, print, or broadcast deliberately false statements that will expose another person to contempt, ridicule, hatred, or financial injury. It is also against the law to blacken the memory of the dead.

There are two kinds of libel. In civil libel, one individual sues another person or company. In criminal libel, the crime is against society and the public or government brings the court action. One who loses a civil libel suit is fined a sum of money which is awarded to the person bringing suit. In a criminal libel suit, the individual losing the case is subject to the same punishment as anyone else committing a crime — in other words, he may be imprisoned.

There is an absolute privilege that protects judges, witnesses, and legislators. They cannot be sued for the things they say when they participate in public proceedings.

2. *Public Officials*

It is very difficult to be charged with libel for written criticism about a public official or a candidate for public office. In 1963 in the case of the *New York Times Company* versus *Sullivan* the Court ruled:

> A defamatory falsehood relating to his official conduct must be made with 'actual malice'...that is, with knowledge that it was false or with reckless disregard of whether it was false or not.

The case itself was very unusual because it concerned an advertisement, and advertisements do not usually come under the protection of freedom of the press. This advertisement, however, printed in the *New York Times,* cited incidents of violations of civil rights in a number of southern cities — among them, Montgomery, Alabama. L. B. Sullivan, a Commissioner of the city of Montgomery, sued four individuals whose names were signed to the advertisement, and the publisher of the *Times.* The lower courts awarded Sullivan libel damages of $500,000.

The Supreme Court reversed the decisions of the lower courts. It held that the newspaper did not forfeit its constitutional guarantee of freedom of the press and criticism of public officials since the comments were made in an "editorial advertisement," not a commercial one.

In the opinion of the court, not to reverse the decision would discourage newspapers from carrying "editorial advertisements …and so might shut off an important outlet for the promulgation of information and ideas by persons who do not themselves have access to publishing facilities…"

Further, the Court stated that "…debate on public issues should be uninhibited, robust, and wide-open, and that it may well include vehement, caustic and sometimes unpleasantly sharp attacks on government and public officials."

3. *Public Figures*

The press has little to fear in libel suits brought by public officials because of the printed or broadcast criticism of those individuals in their official conduct. The issue of freedom to criticize public figures (people whose jobs or civic activities keep them in the public eye) is less clear. In 1967 the Supreme Court decided two cases which provided some answers to this problem.

One was the case of former University of Georgia Athletic Director Wally Butts. In 1963 the *Saturday Evening Post* magazine printed a story which claimed that Butts had given some of his university's football secrets to Alabama Coach Paul Bryant. According to the *Post* story, Butts' action allowed Bryant's team to defeat Georgia in an important football game. Butts sued the *Post* for libel and was awarded close to a half million dollars.

The second case was brought by the Associated Press (AP) which had been sued for libel by former Army Major General Edwin Walker. General Walker had been awarded a $500,000 judgement against the Associated Press. The Associated Press, a news service whose stories go to many papers throughout the United States, was sued for libel by Walker because of an AP story sent out when Walker was present on the University of Mississippi campus during the 1962 riots over the admission of Negro James Meredith. The AP story reported that Walker took charge of the crowd and led students against federal marshals.

Wallace Butts, former athletic director at the University of Georgia. The Supreme Court upheld his $460,000 libel victory against the *Saturday Evening Post,* declaring that the *Post* story was "in no sense hot news" and should have been properly researched.

The Supreme Court upheld the judgement in favor of Wally Butts and reversed the judgement favoring General Walker.

In an opinion of the Court the *Saturday Evening Post* had plenty of time to find out if its story was true, yet had not made the slightest attempt to do so.

In reversing the judgement against the AP the Court said that riot news, because it went to daily papers, had to be sent at once without taking time to check the facts. Supreme Court Justice Harlan said that the AP story would not have seemed unlikely to people previously familiar with public statements by Walker.

While the Supreme Court in the 1960's has developed some tests about the libel of public officials and public figures, many questions remain unanswered. The Court may well be faced with the problem of defining who is a public official and who is a public figure. It may also have to decide when a minor public official (such as a school teacher) is being criticized in his capacity as a government employee and when the criticism is applied to him as a private citizen.

A pressman checking his work.

Roger Baldwin (left), founder of the American Civil Liberties Union, with **John deJ. Pemberton, Jr.**, Executive Director. The ACLU was founded in 1920 in response to wartime and postwar restrictions on speech and press. Its efforts to ensure the First Amendment guarantee of a free press include opposition to censorship and promotion of greater public access to government information. In court cases, the ACLU is represented by lawyers who serve without fee. The ACLU may handle a case directly or may appear as *amicus*, friend of the court.

Conclusion

The story of the press since the founding of the United States has generally been a story of freedom. There have been incidents which have caused the temporary loss of that freedom. The most notable of these were the passage of the Sedition Act of 1798, the World War I restrictions on speech and press, and the McCarthy investigations.

The Supreme Court often answers important questions about the meaning of freedom of the press. Even so, there are certain things about the Supreme Court which should be understood. They are: (1) The Court does not hear all freedom of press cases. Not all lower court decisions are appealed. Even when an appeal is made the Supreme Court can refuse to hear it if it so chooses. (2) The Court often reverses itself. Court members change. Ideas which at times represent the majority in other times represent the minority. The majority decision rules. (3) Supreme Court Justices are only men. The same factors which influence public opinion influence the members of the Court. The Court *usually* gives the people only a little more freedom than they want.

The guarantee of a free press in the Bill of Rights is made meaningful only by the citizens of the United States. If they do not like ideas expressed on television and radio broadcasts they can refuse to buy the sponsor's products and write letters of protest. They also can boycott theaters, newspapers, and magazines.

How much freedom of the press do we want in America? This question must be answered by each individual for himself. And he can only answer it by discovering how much freedom we have now, how much we have had during different periods in the past, and what the results of that freedom (or lack of it) have been.

67

In September 1958 the United States Government issued a postage stamp honoring journalism and freedom of the press. The stamp commemorates the 50th anniversary of the founding of the world's first school of journalism, at the University of Missouri.

...INDEX...

ACKNOWLEDGMENTS

The illustrations are reproduced through the courtesy of: pp. 6, 21, State Historical Society of Wisconsin; pp. 7, 9, 12, 13, 19 (right), 22, 26 (top), 28, 31, 40, 41, 42, 50, 54, 61, Independent Picture Service; p. 10, The Metropolitan Museum of Art, Wolfe Fund, 1931; p. 11, National Portrait Gallery, London; p. 14, The Louvre, Paris, Photo Alinari; p. 16, Yale University; p. 19 (left), The Rare Book Division, The New York Public Library, Astor, Lenox and Tilden Foundations; p. 23, The New York Public Library; pp. 26 (bottom), 27, 30, 33, 36, 37 (right), 58, 60, Library of Congress; pp. 34, 43, Chicago Historical Society; p. 37 (left), St. Louis Post-Dispatch; p. 38, Defense Department, Marine Corps Photo 515603; p. 39, The New York Times; p. 44, Quadrangle Books; p. 48, Harris & Ewing; p. 52, Louisiana State Museum; p. 53, U.S. Army Photograph; p. 55, CBS News Photo; p. 57, Minneapolis Star and Tribune; p. 64, University of Georgia; p. 65, St. Paul Dispatch-Pioneer Press; p. 66, American Civil Liberties Union; p. 68, Post Office Department, Division of Philately.

ABOUT THE AUTHOR

DAVID J. GOLDMAN was born in Chicago, Illinois and grew up in Minneapolis, where he graduated from the University of Minnesota with a B.A. in Journalism. As an undergraduate he helped to organize and publish an independent journal of student opinion. Goldman has done post-graduate work in American History and is enrolled in the University of Minnesota Law School.

The IN AMERICA *Series*

The CZECHS *and* SLOVAKS *in America*
The EAST INDIANS *and* PAKISTANIS *in America*
The ENGLISH *in America*
The FRENCH *in America*
The GERMANS *in America*
The IRISH *in America*
The ITALIANS *in America*
The JAPANESE *in America*
The NEGRO *in America*
The NORWEGIANS *in America*
The SCOTS *and* SCOTCH-IRISH *in America*
The SWEDES *in America*
The FREEDOM OF THE PRESS *in America*
The FREEDOM OF SPEECH *in America*

We specialize in publishing quality books for
young people. For a complete list please write:

LERNER PUBLICATIONS COMPANY
241 First Avenue North, Minneapolis, Minnesota 55401